IGNOSTICISM

A PHILOSOPHICAL JUSTIFICATION FOR ATHEISM

TRISTAN VICK

Hungry Word Publications

Hungry Word Publications presents *Ignosticism A Philosophical Justification for Atheism* by Tristan Vick. All Rights Reserved.

Copyright © 2013 by Tristan Vick

Second Edition: October 1, 2013.

Cover design by Tristan Vick

www.tristanvick.com

ISBN: 1490961828

ISBN-13: 978-1490961828

DEDICATION

For nonbelievers everywhere.

CONTENTS

Better to illuminate than merely to shine, to deliver to others contemplated truths than merely to contemplate.

–St. Thomas Aquinas (*Summa Theologica)*

PREFACE

NOT SO LONG AGO I HAD A DISCUSSION WITH A religious believer online. He expressed a sentiment I have heard expressed often in circles of religious believers who don't quite understand why, or how for that matter, anyone could *not* believe in God. Like many believers, he was under the impression that it must be a personal rebellion against God. That secretly, deep down inside, all nonbelievers really *did* believe—they just couldn't bring themselves to admit it—for whatever reason.

> To even ask the question 'does God exist' requires one to make the a priori assumption that God probably does exist, otherwise the question doesn't make any sense to ask.

Even though my religious friend was seemingly sincere, I couldn't help but laugh to myself at the horribly inaccurate view he held of nonbelievers. Like the psychologist Jesse Bering has pointed out, "One can still enjoy the illusion of God, after all, without believing Him to be real."[1]

I might add, in all fairness, one can even capitalize the pronoun Him, as is common when talking about the monotheistic God of classical theism, without believing it does anything other than help distinguish that deity apart from the thousands of other deities already in existence. I will go one further and say, one may choose to use the Oxford comma simply out of a fondness of the grammatical tradition without believing it's the only comma in existence.

Whether or not we reject a belief as true or false depends on whether or not there is compelling evidence to persuade us either way. The assumption God exists is merely the *theistic* assumption. The assumption God doesn't exist is simply the *atheistic* assumption. The question is which assumption of the two is correct?

If anything, the question "Does God exist?" seems to be weighted in favor of the atheist, because no amount of "belief conviction" or "religious tradition" has ever provided convincing and reliable evidence in the way moderns have come to expect of questions of empirical value. Thus the need for the question.

By refusing to accept even the proposition that others do not believe in God, my online friend refused

---

[1] Jesse Bering, *The Belief Instinct*, p. 8.

to accept the possibility that God may not be real, and so he merely denied this possibility by making up an excuse for why atheists *secretly* believe in God. You see, if everyone believes in God, it would be so much easier to believe in God! Luckily, that's not the case.

Of course I don't know for a fact that god does not exist. There could very well be a god. As for the question of whether or not a god might possibly exist, I remain agnostic. But I have confidence in my cognitive faculties, at least enough so that I would probably recognize compelling evidence if I ever saw it. I know many nonbelievers who say the same. If they saw compelling evidence for the type of God religious believers say exists, well, then there would be no such thing as atheists. In fact, there wouldn't even be any unbelievers. In order to enter into unbelief in something, it first has to be falsified. You don't enter into unbelief for things that are true. As such, what we'd be left with are simply disbelievers.

But the fact of the matter is that atheists do exist. Moreover, atheism is as old as any religion, and equally as viable as any God belief, and this is a detail which often gets overlooked.

The thing is, the reasons atheists typically do not believe in the gods of religion is, first and foremost, the lack of compelling evidence. Secondly, it seems that we have a naturalistic explanation for the origin of religion. Modern psychology has explained, rather well I might add, how religion works at the level of the mind. Social anthropologists have compared notes and have come to the realization that the religions of the world all share things in common with each other because humans are the originators of religion, and therefore the indelible stamp of human fingerprints are all over religion. More recently still, neuroscientists have peered into the brains of believers, as well as nonbelievers, to see what is going on at the fundamental levels of belief. Surprisingly, in many cases both believers and nonbeliever prove to be equally superstitious. Evolutionary psychology and science have provided us with a physical, naturalistic, account for how religion arises.

Most atheists and nonbelievers aren't puzzled by the existence of religion. We are fairly confident that we know how religion arises. What's more is that we're pretty certain these are entirely natural explanations and nothing is out of the ordinary with respect to how one acquires religious belief. What we are confused about is how people, with access to this same information which elucidates the origins of religious belief, continue to believe in something which, to the nonbeliever, appears to either be made on bad reasoning or else has been demonstrated as flagrantly false.

I for one want to know what people mean when they say they believe in God, because in my experience, people rarely ever mean the same thing by it. God means something different to everyone.

Of course they may not say so in the presence of

other believers, agreeing when they are in the company of like-minded people of faith, such as when they are paying lip service to God at church, [2] but having talked with religious believers quite extensively, both in person and online, I have learned that they rarely describe their experience of God in the same way.

Perhaps the final reason which nonbelievers do not hold belief in God is the fact that many view belief in God as akin to belief in Santa Claus. This comparison isn't meant as an insult to believers, but reveals an uncanny similarity in the way delusions can infiltrate and get a hold on your mind. When it comes to complex ideas and concepts that require us to use the analytical parts of our brains, it seems better critical thinking

---

[2] It seems group conformity and the halo effect are much stronger influences than most people think, especially with regard to religious belief in God. In some studies nearly 70% of people agreed with erroneous information simply because a rigged majority confirmed the fallacy as true. In other studies, people would agree with false information if it was repeated more than three times. People will also follow the consensus, even when they know beforehand that the consensus is wrong. See: Sherif, M. (1935) "A study of some social factors in perception," Archives of Psychology, 27 (187), pp.17-22. Also see: Asch, S.E. (1951), "Effects of group pressure upon the modification and distortion of judgment," In H. Guetzkow (ed.) Groups, leadership and men. Pittsburgh, PA: Carnegie Press. As well as: Asch, S.E. (1955), "Opinions and social pressure," Scientific American, 193 (5), pp. 31-35. Finally, see: Berns, G.S., et all (2005), "Neurobiological Correlates of Social Conformity and Independence During Mental Rotation," Biological Psychiatry, 58 (3), pp.245-253.

skills are to be desired. [3]

Like any skill critical thinking takes practice to do well. Being smart isn't the same as being rational. Isaac Newton, who is considered by many to be one of the smartest minds who has ever lived, still held onto superstitious falsities. In his off hours of not inventing calculus and figuring out the basic forces of nature, he was an alchemist. [4] So even super smart people can still hold extremely irrational beliefs.

I've met many smart religious believers as well as many irrational nonbelievers. Even so, seeing as how religion infiltrates the mind of the young early on, causing most peoples' understanding of God to be like that of a child's, for the person who grows out of religion and learns to think about all the complexities of life, you might say, we have learned to put childish things behind us. We have simply outgrown God belief.

But this doesn't mean that the phenomenon of

---

[3] The analytical function of the brain is commonly referred to as *System 2*. The more intuitive thinking part of the brain is referred to as *System 1*. To learn more on the differences between the two systems, read: *Thinking, Fast and Slow* by Daniel Kahneman. Farrar, Straus and Giroux, New York, 2011.

[4] Interestingly enough, in addition to alchemy, Isaac Newton was also a Anti-trinitarian monotheist. What this means is that, although he believed in a supreme deity, he didn't believe Jesus Christ was divine or at all related to that deity. In fact, Newton believed that worshiping Jesus Christ as the son of God was a form of idolatry. See: Snobelen, Stephen D. (1999). "Isaac Newton, heretic: the strategies of a Nicodemite" (PDF). *British Journal for the History of Science* 32 (4): 381–419. PDF available online at: http://www.isaac-newton.org/heretic.pdf

religious belief doesn't still entice us. As humans with a vested interest in what humans think and do, how could we not be interested in religion?

As you might have guessed, I find the topic of religion a truly fascinating subject. So much so that I have made it a habit to try and understand religion in light of my own deconversion process from three decades of pious Christian faith. By understanding how my religious beliefs have impacted me, I can better critique other religious experiences, ideas, and claims. The reason I feel this is a worthwhile endeavor is not because I am some kind of big bad atheist out to rid the world of religion, but rather, I think that if others understood religion at a fundamental level then they would not be prone to make the mistakes which are commonly made by those under the influence of religion.

Mistakes such as professing those who do *not* believe in God must (somehow) *secretly* believe in God. Mistakes like thinking a child's theology would somehow pertain to adult experience or that an adult's theology could supposedly be comprehended by a child. Mistakes like believing God doesn't want you to vaccinate your children or that magic invocations of prayer would work equally as well as medical treatment by highly trained medical professionals.

These are not mistakes people would make if they had a better understanding of religion and exercised a little bit more discernment in the beliefs they accept as constituting true representations of reality. These aforementioned examples are mistakes that can only be made if a person takes their religion and religious beliefs for granted.

In this book I have taken steps to try and make sense of and understand God from a different perspective than traditional religious devotional faith. As a nonbeliever, this book serves as one possible explanation for why God probably does not exist and so, subsequently, is one argument (of many) for why I do not believe.

Although it's not meant to be an academic work, some of the concepts are challenging, and if I make mistakes it is most assuredly due to my own limitations. Then again, I have given it my best, and if other people find my arguments compelling or beneficial, then great. But please do not mistake this book as a scornful criticism of God and religious faith. It's not meant as one. Rather, it's meant as a philosophical objection to theistic belief, and perhaps, in the process, if we happen to find ample reasons that support atheism and validate a position nonbelief, then so be it.

Tristan Vick

July 10, 2013

INTRODUCTION

I TAKE A *CONSTRUCTIVIST* APPROACH TO THE theory of knowing whether or not God exists. Constructivism is an area of learning theory and epistemology which holds the position that

> 1) We have to focus on the learner in thinking about learning (not on the subject/lesson to be taught).
>
> 2) There is no knowledge independent of the meaning attributed to experience (constructed) by the learner, or community of learners. [5]

Professor Hein of Lesley College, Massachusetts,

---

[5] George E. Hein, "Constructivist Learning Theory," presented at the CECA conference, Israel, 1991. Available online at:

http://www.exploratorium.edu/ifi/resources/constructivistlearning.html

has detailed the premise of constructivism more succinctly, stating:

> There is no such thing as knowledge "out there" independent of the knower, but only knowledge we construct for ourselves as we learn. Learning is not understanding the "true" nature of things, nor is it (as Plato suggested) remembering dimly perceived perfect ideas, but rather a personal and social construction of meaning out of the bewildering array of sensations which have no order or structure besides the explanations (and I stress the plural) which we fabricate for them.[6]

Those who hold different epistemological views often tend to dismiss constructivism off hand, taking a more Platonic view of knowledge. However, this ignores the latest support constructivist theories have gained in the blossoming field of cognitive science.[7]

In his seminal work *Philosophical Investigations*, the language theorist Ludwig Wittgenstein regularly

---

[6] Ibid.

[7] Constructivism has far-reaching consequences for the study of cognitive development and learning. One of the principles is that knowledge is not passively received but actively built up by the experiential world, not the discovery of an ontological reality. See: *Leslie P. Steffe, Jerry Gale, "Constructivism in Education," Routledge,* 2012.

referred to the concept of *language-games*. According to Wittgenstein, language doesn't necessarily have a direct connection to reality, and he argued that concepts do not need to be so clearly defined in order to be meaningful.[8]

Wittgenstein used the term "language-game" to designate forms of language simpler than the entirety of a language itself, "consisting of language and the actions into which it is woven" (PI 7), and connected by *family resemblance*.

What the term family resemblance refers to are things that may be thought to be connected by one essential common feature might in fact be connected by a series of overlapping similarities, where no one feature is common to all. Games in general, like chess and checkers, were used by Wittgenstein as an example to better illustrate the notion of language-games, and have become the paradigmatic example of a group that is related by family resemblances.

The concept of an ongoing language-game was intended "to bring into prominence the fact that the speaking of language is part of an activity, or a form of life…" (PI 23). Wittgenstein's theories, I think you'll find, are fully compatible with constructivist thought regarding language.

When it comes to the idea of God my thinking is

---

[8] Note: Even so, unclearly defined concepts may still prove incoherent and therefore problematic.

that God is a product of a type of language-game. That is, the very definition itself—"God"—is not a description of any ontological reality, nor an explanation, but rather a type of language-based construction. In other words, a highly innovative conceptualization rooted in the process and function of human based language-games.

Usually God-conceptualizations are part of a collaborative group process. In fact, it would not be wrong to say that God is a social concept constructed by groups of people (not individuals). Very few individuals have created their own complex theologies—and those that have, such as Joseph Smith and L. Ron Hubbard, have formulated conceptualizations which could not have thrived if it wasn't for the group effort to support and maintain them in a way that relates back to a type of social constructivism. [9]

Social constructivism, strongly influenced by the Russian social psychologist Lev Vygotsky's (1978), suggests that knowledge is first constructed in a social context and is then taken up by individuals. [10]

---

[9] It seems that many God-conceptualizations rely on an innovative process of formulation that is predicted by what is referred to as a *Knowledge Spiral*. See the research of Nonaka Takeuchi, "The Knowledge-Creating Company - How Japanese Companies Create the Dynamics of Innovation," New York; Oxford, 1995.

[10] Also see: Bruning et al., 1999; M. Cole, 1991; Eggan and Kauchak, 2004.

According to social constructivists like Vygotsky, the process of sharing each person's point of view—called *collaborative elaboration*—results in learners building understanding together that wouldn't be possible alone.

It seems to me that constructivism and language-games work together to create systems which look a lot like how God belief within religion functions and how I experienced religion when I was a dyed in the wool believer. [11] If this is true, then it seems to suggest that the idea of God does not represent any part of reality but rather exists merely as a construct of the human imagination.

---

[11] I need not go out of my way, I do not think, to defend constructivism too vigorously as it is a well-established and respected epistemology. Additionally, modern neuroscience research has affirmed many constructivist theories about learning. See: James Zull, *The art of changing the brain: Enriching the practice of teaching by exploring the biology of learning.* Sterling, VA: Stylus Publishing, L.L.C., 2002. Also see: "Cognitive development," In A. Demetriou, W. Doise, K. F. M. van Lieshout (Eds.), *Life-span developmental psychology* (pp. 179-269), London: Wiley, 1998. Also see: Demetriou, Andreas, and Athanassios Raftopoulos. "Modeling the Developing Mind: From Structure to Change." *Developmental Review* 19 (1999): 319-368.

1

IGNOSTICISM

A S A GENTLEMAN PHILOSOPHER—ONE WHO studies philosophy informally simply for the love of philosophy—I have gradually learned to defend my beliefs and construct sturdy arguments in favor of them. But I am not beyond checking my own beliefs. One of the things which I strive for in my own personal philosophy is to constantly hone my critical thinking and reasoning skills. Subsequently, I have grown ever skeptical of religious faith-based propositions and have gradually come to the belief that atheism can be more rigorously defended than any theistic belief system. Moreover, I believe this is a defensible claim.

What follows is a summation of what I feel is one of the strongest knock-down arguments against the existence of God I have ever run across. Mind you, there are other philosophical arguments worth considering as well, such as the Problem of Evil and the Problem of Divine Hiddenness.[12] [13] Like these other strong arguments against the existence of supernatural deities, the argument I present here can be toted as an equally worthy disproof for God and, subsequently, support for an atheistic worldview. That is, believe it or not, it is a positive claim for the reasonableness of a lack of belief in God. It is known simply as *Ignosticism*.

Plainly stated *ignosticism* (sometimes called *igtheism*)[14] is a position, first outlined by the Jewish humanist rabbi Sherwin Wine, that views the question of God's existence as meaningless, because nearly all definitions of God prove incoherent when held up to exacting scrutiny. Consequently, arguing about the existence of God also becomes meaningless because having no coherent definition for "God" it becomes unclear what we are supposed to be arguing exists.

---

[12] For a thorough summation of the Problem of Evil visit the *Stanford Encyclopedia of Philosophy* at: http://plato.stanford.edu/entries/evil/

[13] Meanwhile, J.L. Schellenberg has discussed the problem of Divine Hiddenness at length. See: "Would a Loving God Hide from Anyone?" In Solomon, Robert; McDermid, Douglas. Introducing Philosophy for Canadians, 2011. Oxford University Press. pp. 165–166. Extended notes from Schellenberg's 2011 St. Thomas Summer Seminar about the Hiddenness arguments for atheism can be read online at:

http://www.jlschellenberg.com/recent-notes-on-divine-hiddenness.html

[14] The term *igtheism* was coined by humanist Paul Kurtz in his 1992 book *The New Skepticism*.

At the same time, ignosticism is closely related to *Theological noncognitivism* which takes the view that the sentence "God exists" is cognitively meaningless.[15] In a nut shell, the theological noncognitivist claims that all alleged definitions for the term "God" amount to the same thing as "God is that which caused everything but God," which "defines God in terms of God," thus amounts to circular reasoning.

Philosopher of Religion and Professor emeritus at West Virginia University Theodore Drange has stated the problem more concisely when he informs us that

> Since the word "God" has many different meanings, it is possible to express many different propositions. What we need to do is to focus on each proposition separately. ... For each different sense of the term "God," there will be theists, atheists, and agnostics *relative* to that concept of God.[16]

---

[15] Steven J. Conifer of Marshall University has written a detailed explication of theological noncognitivism, entitled "Theological Noncognitivism Examined," which can be read online at:

http://web.archive.org/web/20090326144947/http://www.sewanee.edu/philosophy/Journal/Archives/2002/Conifer.htm

[16] From the article "Atheism, Agnosticism, Noncognitivism" by Theodore Drange (1998). Available online at:

http://www.infidels.org/library/modern/theodore_drange/definition.html

Before we delve into a deeper discussion about a little known, even less talked about, philosophical consideration, it would help us to lay down a working description of ignosticism and its parts. Accordingly, ignosticism holds two interrelated views about God. They are as follows:

1) A coherent definition of God must be presented before the question of the existence of God can be meaningfully discussed.

2) If the definition provided is unfalsifiable (e.g., God is *transcendent*), the ignostic takes the theological noncognitivist position that the question of the existence of God is meaningless.[17]

Keeping these above considerations in mind, we will begin our discussion on how ignosticism might be applied and how it lends positive support to the atheistic worldview. After briefly laying out a basic description of ignosticism and how it works, we will discuss some of its consequences and possible objections.

---

[17] There seems to be some concern surrounding the question as to whether or not arbitrarily assigned definitions in themselves can be falsifiable. I address this question regarding *semantics* in chapter five.

2

PROBLEM OF DISSIMILARITY

IF I WERE TO BE STOPPED ON THE STREET today by a religious person and they asked whether or not I believed in God, my response would simply be, "What do you mean?"

Contrary to what you might think, I am not trying to be a smart aleck. In earnest, I would literally be asking them what they meant by the term "God." Now, this might sound strange at first. After all, doesn't everyone have a basic understanding of what God is? If so, shouldn't we know what is meant by the question?

The answer is no. You see, it's not so simple. Although we gain our understanding of God through culture, tradition, and reflection, the question of whether or not we believe in something's existence only makes sense if what we are being asked to believe in makes sense. The greater question underlying the previous question is, "Does the term 'God' make sense?" In other words, is the definition coherent?

If we cannot understand what it is we are being asked to believe in, then we have a serious problem. For example, if I asked you, "Do you believe in Twinkerschwetzles?" then you'd be perfectly justified in asking me, "What do you mean by Twinkerschwetzles?"

In order to make you understand what a "Twinkerschwetzle" is, I'd have to describe and explain it to you. Likewise, in order to make us understand what "God" is, people of faith have the responsibility to describe and explain what it is they mean by "God."

That isn't to say that most definitions of God don't make sense. To the contrary, they make perfect sense to the person who believes in that particular conceptualization of God. But with the caveat that specific conceptualizations tend to usually only make sense within the confines of that religious belief system (and those directly related to it). For example, although a Christian, Jew, and Muslim might agree upon the definition of God, if you asked an aborigine from the Australian outback, or a native of Papua New Guinea, or a Native American of the Great Plains, they would all probably give you very different descriptions of what "God" is to them.

Everyone has their own unique concept of God. But herein lays the problem. As the anthropologist Pascal Boyer has observed in his book *Religion*

Explained, "Not all possible concepts are equally good. The ones we acquire easily are the ones we find widespread the world over."[18]

Boyer goes on to describe the various types of God beliefs people regularly hold, informing:

> Supernatural agents can be very different. Religion is about the existence and causal powers of non-observable entities and agencies. These may be one unique God or many different ones or spirits or ancestors or any combination of these different kinds.[19]

So from the start the very definition of "God" is complicated by the numerous conceptualizations of what a term like "God" entails.

Another observation we can make is that once we step outside of that particular brand of religious faith, the believer's definition of God ceases to have and relevant meaning. Those who have their own definitions for "God" would simply deny competing definitions that didn't comport with their own.

Perhaps even more problematic still is the fact that even within the very same religion there may be various interpretations of the same God. Sometimes these

---

[18] Pascal Boyer, *Religion Explained* (2001), p. 4

[19] Ibid., p. 7

interpretations grow shockingly dissimilar, and can sometimes even lead to conflicting definitions of, supposedly, the same God.

Christianity is a prime example of a religion capable of housing numerous simultaneous, yet differing, interpretations of God under the same umbrella of religious faith. The proliferation of Christian denominations, each of them professing a slightly different theological view of God, and thus providing slightly different descriptions as a result, have the incontrovertible problem of having to account for these differences for what it is they mean by "God."

A God which commands his followers to hate homosexuals, for example, cannot be the same God who simultaneously commands his followers to love homosexuals. By their very definitions the terms love and hate are antonymous. Yet these are the very descriptions provided by Fundamentalist and Liberal branches of Christian faith for presumably the same God. As such, the definition of the Christian God becomes incoherent when we try to reconcile the various competing definitions within the faith itself. This is what I call the *Problem of dissimilarity.*

It is peculiar to the outsider that a group which devotes so much time to the study of a single entity could not, at end of the day, agree on a definition of it even as they all profess a ubiquitous belief in it. Putting this peculiarity aside though, what should remain clear is the fact that Christians still haven't agreed on what even their own definition of "God" means—even as they profess belief in their version of God.

Different descriptions give rise to different definitions, however. Indeed, the very purpose of a description is to provide an accurate definition. If anything should clear to us, it is that out of the varieties of Christians they do *not* all believe in the same God. Christians believe in very different conceptualizations of what they profess to be the same God. But until they can resolve the problem of dissimilarity, their definitions of "God" are simply incoherent.

In fact, if you look at all the competing definitions of God which exist in the world, or have ever existed, it will become abundantly clear to you that most definitions of the various deities are radically different from one another.[20] So much so that the definitions provided seem impossible to reconcile.

---

[20] On the website *Graveyard of the Gods*, Francois Tremblay provides an extensive list of thousands of dead or forgotten gods which used to be actively worshipped which no longer are. You can find the list online at:

http://www.graveyardofthegods.org/deadgods/listofgods.html

3

OSTENSIBLE ATTRIBUTES

ONE QUESTION WHICH ARISES IS WHY should the definitions of God/gods turn out to be different at all? It goes without saying there are anthropological, cultural, as well as geographical reasons for these seemingly unavoidable variations in God belief. Different cultures lend to different outlooks. It comes down to how a person frames their experience and how they make sense of their understanding of this experience.

Likewise, we will often frame our experiences within the confines of our cultural beliefs. As it happens, many of these cultural beliefs are indistinguishable from religious ones, as in many parts of the world there is no distinction to be made between culture and religious culture. They are, in many cases, one and the same thing.

This proves to be problematic for the reason that in most parts of the world people start with the definition of God which has already been fully supplied by the thread of common experience that exists within their religious faith and cultural worldview.

Having an already established definition for what God means, according to one's cultural experiences, sounds perfectly fine when everyone shares a like-minded belief. Many Catholics preach God *is* love, because that's what Catholics ubiquitously believe. But asking the question "Is God love" forces us to come to a realization that the term "love" has merely been ascribed to God, not derived from God. Christian theology supplies the definition, not from the study of God, but from what the Holy Bible says about God. So already we have a cultural and religious worldview providing the believer with a specific definition of God, in this case, that God is love.

Bear in mind, however, that most descriptions of God are not even proper descriptions. Rather, they are just additional "names" (often culturally derived) ascribed to whatever *thing* people might imagine "God" to be. The question then becomes, are Catholics truly describing God or are they describing the God they derived from their interpretation of the Bible, hundreds of years of theology, and pious imagination? Have we been given a description of God or merely a Catholic name for God? The answer is quite simply that we've merely been given the Catholic name for God. If it were an accurate description of God, then every other Christian would profess belief in the exact same God, and their definition of God would be the same. But this we do not find. The Calvinist variety of Christianity, for example, believes in a God which will predestine people to hell. This could never be a perfectly loving being since such a God is far too capricious. As such, we know that Catholics and Calvinists are not describing the same entity, but rather, are merely naming their individual version of God as either *loving* or *deterministic*.

Likewise, the three great monotheisms of Judaism, Christianity, and Islam are said to all stem from the Abrahamic faith. As such, they all claim to believe in the same God, the God of Abraham. But low and behold, their definitions of this God vary drastically.

Christians positively claim that God begot a Son, Jesus Christ, whereas Muslims affirm that God does not beget Sons—no way, no how. Right off the bat we must grow suspicious of the discrepancies in God's character (after all, this is supposed to be the *exact same deity we are talking about).

So if it's the same God, then why are the descriptions of him dissimilar? Dissimilar descriptions, as we have seen, lead to divergent definitions. In the case of the competing definitions regarding the Christian and Islamic conceptions of God, we find the very definition of God rendered incoherent. God cannot both beget a son and not beget a son simultaneously. It is logically incoherent, in the same way the term a "married bachelor" is a logically incoherent definition.

It wasn't until I read the Austrian philosopher Ludwig Wittgenstein that this practice of 'naming' a thing instead of 'describing' a thing started to bother me with respect to the idea of God. According to Wittgenstein:

> Naming and describing do not stand on the same level: naming is a preparation for describing. Naming is not a move in a language game—any more than putting a piece in its place on the board is a move in chess. One may say: with the mere naming of a thing, nothing has yet been done.[21]

So why is this a problem for the person who believes in God? Well, it comes down to the realization that in most cases the definitions people give for God are not proper definitions. That is, they are not 'descriptions' of God but rather 'names' applied to a specific conceptualization. The religious anthropologist Pascal Boyer calls these religious conceptualizations *templates*, and identifies a list of ones which are commonly shared among the world's religions. Regarding these religious templates he states:

---

[21] Wittgenstein, *Philosophical Investigations*, p.28e. Wiley-Blackwell, 2009.

> Religious representations are particular combinations of mental representations that satisfy two conditions. First, the religious concepts *violate* certain expectations from ontological categories. Second, they *preserve* other expectations.[22]

Boyer then gives a list of template examples. Number twenty-one from the list is: Omniscient God [PERSON] = *special cognitive powers*. This example illustrates one possible template, and is one of many possible religious representations of God.

Now if a theologian imbues his sense of God with metaphysical characteristics, such as saying that God is transcendent, all-loving, omniscient, omnipresent, immutable, eternal, existing outside of space and time, well, these are just the various templates which other theists and theologians will use to check their definitions of God against.

As a consequence of having preconceived templates, however, the religious believer hasn't provided a reliable description of anything extant and nothing has been done yet to provide a meaningful definition. As Wittgenstein said, naming and describing are different things. All the theist has done here, technically speaking, is attach alternative names to their unique conceptualization of God (e.g., a Catholic *loving*

---

[22] Pascal Boyer, *Religion Explained*, p. 62

God vs. a Calvinist *deterministic* God) and thus, in this act of naming, have developed a highly stylized template.

Another example of ritualistic 'naming' exists within Islamic faith. According to Muslim tradition, Allah has 99 holy names.

> Abu Hurairah reported Allah's Messenger (may peace be upon him) as saying: There are ninety-nine names of Allah; he who commits them to memory would get into Paradise.[23]

Having come to the realization that most religious definitions of God come from a tradition of naming and not via any valid description, we come to see that nearly all definitions of God are ostensible.[24] We find that it is simply another case of putting the cart before the horse. Consequently, this supports the ignostic claim that the theist is assuming to know too much about God.

---

[23] Muslim ibn al-Hajjaj Nishapuri, *Sahih Muslim*, 35:6475.

[24] I say *nearly all definitions of God are ostensible since, technically speaking, not all definitions of God are ostensible. A child's definition of God, for example, would be overly simplistic (predictably anthropomorphic) because of the limitations of child psychology and a young person's inability to grasp complex theological concepts. Instead of their definition of God being ostensible, their definition would be inadequate. See: Michael Martin, *Atheism: A Philosophical Justification*, p. 45. Temple University Press, 1990.

4

REFERENTIAL JUSTIFICATION

A LTHOUGH IGNOSTICISM CONCERNS ITSELF WITH the coherence of definitions, traditional ignosticism lacks any formal method of justification. Now what is a *justification*, you might wonder? According to the Oxford Dictionary of Philosophy a justification is:

> An action or a belief that stands up to some kind of critical reflection or scrutiny; a person is then exempt from criticism on account of it. The philosophical question is one of the standards that have to be met and the source of their authority.

Without any justification, ignosticism would not be capable of making the claim of incoherence for God, but since the claim of ignosticism is that some terms are coherent while others are not, it stems to reason we need a method for checking which is which.

Knowing descriptions that accurately reflect an object or thing lead to coherent definitions, we can seek to find a method of authenticating something by looking closely at its description. In this case, by examining its *referent* since descriptions of real world things must be about referents. Descriptions of concepts and ideas, on the other hand, will be described in terms of other concepts and ideas. As such, I have devised a system of justification, what I call *Referential justification,* to help us navigate these semantic waters.

Now, what is Referential justification exactly? Well, it's simply this. By analyzing a things description we can better determine whether it is relating to something within reality or not. If so, our definition will align lending to coherency, if not, then incoherency.

Something that exists in reality (i.e., the object or the thing itself) in which a description can be derived is called a *referent.* Conversely, we also have *concepts.* Concepts are things that are based on ideas, and need not necessarily relate back to something which exists in reality.[25]

One way to identify whether or not we are dealing with an real world referent or just a concept is to look at

---

[25] In this *reality* refers to the observable natural world, since it is the once we can check all descriptions against. As such, anyone can use this test to justify the validity of their descriptions thereby lending to the credence of their derived terms.

how the thing itself is defined. If it's defined using other ideas, analogies, and terms that invoke metaphysical language then it's probably a concept. If it's defined by describing its details as observed or measured, often through sensate description, then it's likely something experiential and therefore tangible. It's the difference between an *object* and an *idea*.

In order to prove beyond a reason of a doubt that God is something real, and not just an intricate conceptualization, we must first verify that our description is about something extant.

When believers claim "God exists" for example, we instantly have a claim affirming that God is something extant—i.e., something which presently exists. If so, and God is real, then a referent must exist for the object "God" to be considered real. From this object a description can be derived.

Upon realizing we lack any tangible referent for God however, we have no choice but to reevaluate whether or not God really exists. Without a verified referent, God seems to devolve into a concept. Theists aware of this change from *real* to *conceptual* will often resort to re-defining God in metaphysical terms. This is part of the semantic gymnastics believers frequently employ when they cannot describe God according to the standards of what constitutes a formal definition of an object (we'll discuss semantic confusion more in depth in the next chapter).

So what about those who claim God is beyond

space and time, that he exists external to our reality, but somehow resides in some metaphysical relationship to it? I think my friend Mike D., author of the popular blog *The A-Unicornist*, stated it best, informing:

> The fact remains that gods may exist beyond our epistemic horizon. This makes them irrelevant, but since probability is merely a description of possible scenarios within our physical reality, it's meaningless to talk about whether those 'supernatural' things are probable or not. They're simply indeterminable ... So it's meaningless to talk about whether its claims are probable unless they make a specific falsifiable claim.[26]

If no extant object can be isolated for God, then it means that "God" is not an object that exists in reality, and we are left without a referent, therefore our description is rendered invalid. Existing outside of reality is the same as existing outside of comprehension. As Mike observed, if God/gods do exist beyond our epistemic horizon, it would still be meaningless to talk about the probability of their existence, because probabilities only apply to the

---

[26] Mike D. has written an excellent defense for metaphysical naturalism. In it he explains how metaphysical descriptions of God cannot be meaningful. See his article: "A Slow Crawl Toward Ontological Naturalism," available online at:

http://www.theaunicornist.com/2011/04/slow-crawl-toward-ontological.html

physical reality we observe and experience.[27] Placing God outside of reality does not safeguard God, but does the opposite by making God that much harder to define as anything intelligible and so that much more implausible.

Referential justification is founded on the empirical principle that if we are describing the exact same object within reality, then our descriptions of that object will always match up. This allows us to test the referent against other descriptions of it, thereby justifying the validity of our own previous description.

On the other hand, if our descriptions for the same object do not match up then there is either a problem in the way one of us is perceiving the information, or there is a problem with the information itself.

So what is Referential justification good for? Well, once we verify our descriptions as accurate we can justify belief that the definition we are using is actually about what we believe it to be about. As such, we will be able to better identify coherent and incoherent definitions.

To help us understand this process in more detail, I prefer to use the analogy of comparing our experience of eating a Granny Smith apple. Let's assume that I picked up such an apple at the local supermarket. Now

---

[27] It's work noting that the probability of God's existence within the real physical world has been calculated to be so low as for God to be virtually non-existent. See: Michael Martin and Ricki Monnier's collection: *The Improbability of God*, Prometheus Books, 2006.

we all know what apples feel and taste like regardless of what we call them. This is because we know apples exist in reality, and if there was ever any doubt as to the properties of an apple, all we would have to do is go fetch an apple and take turns examining it.

So let us imagine I have a Granny Smith apple and, pulling out my pocket-knife, I cut the apple in half. Next, giving you one half and keeping the other half for myself, we both bite into our respective halves. Letting the fruit's juices flood into my mouth, I might describe the apple as: *crunchy, juicy,* and *sour.* You, doing the same, would most likely come up with the exact same description. *Crunchy. Juicy. Sour.*

Both of us have agreed that this Granny Smith green apple is crunchy, juicy, and slightly sour. The reason our descriptions match up exactly is because we are deriving our definition from the exact same referent—the thing itself.

Supposing our descriptions did not match however, yet we had the same referent in hand, then we have two possible considerations. Either someone is lying about what the Granny Smith apple is like, or they are mistaken. The point is, we would detect the discrepancy immediately. All we would have to do in order to settle the matter of dissimilarity is bring in a third party and have them taste the apple and then see whose description theirs lines up with.

Green. Crunchy. Juicy. Sour. Granny Smith apple.

This agreement in our independent descriptions

should arise naturally if there is a tangible referent that can act as a unifying reference of experience—the thing itself. If not, and we keep coming across dissimilar descriptions, then we would be clued into the fact that we are probably not dealing with an object that has a referent, but rather, a conceptualization.

What does referential justification mean in terms of belief in God? Well, in order for God to be more than a manmade abstraction there would have to be an agreed upon referent from which we could derive a corresponding description. Since most definitions and descriptions of God do not match up, and are wildly divergent, this lack of similitude suggests that there is no such referent and therefore no genuine reference of shared experience. If there was, we'd find the descriptions of God provided by believers lining up as surely as a compass points north.

Subsequently, this failure to find congruency in our terms helps explain why there are so many divergent descriptions and definitions for God, thereby lending to an ever growing range of diverse conceptualizations being created in the minds of believers. The more diversity there is for supposedly the same thing, the more discrepancies arise, and the more likely the term will be rendered incoherent.

Being a conceptualization based on subjective religious experience then, and not of the thing itself, this diversity is to be expected. It would be a lot like me trying to imagine what a Granny Smith apple tasted like, having never previously tasted one, only for you to come along and explain to me that you imagine a Granny Smith apple tasting another way, having never tasted one. Instead of having the unifying experience of having tasted the Granny Smith apple ourselves, in which our experience of the object of a Granny Smith apple would match up, we would only have our conceptualizations of what a Granny Smith apple might *possibly* taste like.

If God is something that exists in reality then referential justification places the burden squarely on the believer to justify their descriptions of God, demonstrating they are derived from a real shared experience of the thing itself rather than an idea, and thereby provide a reliable and coherent definition which matches and which we can then use to talk about God.

Unable to do so, however, dissimilitude of experience would lead to incongruent descriptions and abstractions would abound. Nobody would know what they were talking about, and this effectively puts us right back at the problem of dissimilarity and the issue of incoherency arises all over again.

5

Semantics

SEMANTICS DOES NOT MEAN WORD GAMES. Rather, semantics is the study of words and how they function in language. Semantics is a valid area of *semiotics*, the study of symbols and language, and deals specifically with the relation between a sign (symbol/word) and its object when discussing the validity of definitions and their meanings.

First off, I feel it would do us some good to address one potential area of confusion which arises with regard to the question of whether or not definitions in themselves can be considered falsifiable, as this is one of the claims of ignosticism that needs to be met in order for ignosticism to be a valid position. I hold that definitions are falsifiable in at least two ways.

A word's definition can either be shown to not accurately relate to the thing it's trying to describe, or a word's meaning can be rendered incomprehensible by a flood of new meanings which seek to confuse us as to the term's purported usage within any given context.

A *definition*, by definition, is an exact description or meaning given to a thing or idea. So if we cannot derive a proper description or cannot settle on a comprehensible meaning, then the term is likely erroneous. Therefore any application of an erroneous term would lead to an invalid, false, description or meaning and would rightly be rejected. But how might we go about detecting erroneous definitions? This requires us to engage in a bit of *semantics*.

Now, it is well understood that many definitions are simply assigned to a thing or idea and the description, more often than not, comes later. That is, we construct the meaning and description of things (e.g., constructivism). But even the arbitrary assignment of a definition, regardless of the tentative meaning, will still require that tentative meaning to match exactly to what it purports to be defining. If it did not, then there is a semantics problem which we need to identify.

Holding any word to its dictionary meaning is, perhaps, too much of a black and white way of looking at the organic, ever changing, nature of human language. Words can often take on additional meanings, as well as jettison meanings, or altogether shift meanings. What semantics asks is whether these definitions and meanings relate back to what they are attempting to describe.

Consider the word *smart*, for example. It can mean both intelligent and attractive. Likewise the word *cool* can mean both good-looking and denote the range between warm and cold temperature.

"The boy is *cool* looking" and "The weather outside is *cool* today" are both easily understood because the dual meaning of the term "cool" is easily understood by English speakers. To the non-native speaker of English however, such dual meanings, which are usually confined to cultural contexts, can often prove to be highly confusing. Therefore, whenever the meaning becomes unclear we automatically try to describe what we mean by giving examples of how the word is used in various contexts.

Dictionaries, as you may have noticed, arrange the meanings of words according to their most relevant usages. So you have your primary meanings listed first, the secondary meanings listed second, and so on and so forth. Even so, these meanings are still coherent, because they can be used in contexts which describe something relatable to that term.

If I were to tell you "The boy rode his bike at a cool pace to school" you would instantly catch the implied meaning of *cool pace*—meaning a leisurely pace—given the context. If I said "The boy rode his bike to school cool" you probably would become a little confused as to what I mean by "cool" since the word's meaning, in this case, cannot be inferred by the context or by the various understood usages of the term.

When confusion like this arises we call it a *semantic confusion*. Semantic confusions arise from either unclear usage of a term's meaning or too many competing meanings where it becomes unclear as to how the word applies to its subject. Typically, semantic confusion is an indicator that we've either used a word incorrectly, or we have forced it to have a new *lexical meaning* which isn't recognized as one which fits within the *semantic field*.[28]

This isn't to say that creating new definitions is wrong, but if you shift a words definition then you must work to maintain that definition according to the way you are seeking to use it and, moreover, you will need to explain how it pertains to the context in which you are using it.

If you shift the word's meaning again, then it is clear that you're employing a semantic confusion where you are free to re-assign the meaning to any given context, and if this is the case, then you probably aren't so much concerned with providing a coherent definition for others to comprehend. But herein lays the problem with semantic confusion. If you are deliberately making your term incomprehensible, then it's not about anything, and therefore cannot be a proper definition.

Now that we have learned how to identify semantic

---

[28] A *lexical meaning* is the meaning of a word considered in isolation from the sentence containing it, and regardless of its grammatical context. A *semantic field* is a lexical set of semantically related items.

confusion when we see it, let's move forward and discuss the difference between definitions which are derived via accurate descriptions of an object that exists in the real world and definitions which are applied to concepts and ideas.

When a theoretical physicist uses the descriptor *string theory* to explain the area of focus they are investigating, we know they are talking about mathematical concepts only, because there is no evidential support that the models predicted in string theory represent any form of reality. To talk about a "string" in string theory, for example, is to talk about a *mathematical construct*. What's more, it is to talk about a concept that is, so far, without a referent in reality. As any honest physicist would tell you, strings haven't been confirmed by observation or experiment yet. All we have are the word associations and maths that help us build up the concept of strings by analogy. They exist only as abstractions. More specifically, they exist only as abstractions in the minds of theoretical physicists.

When we are talking about a diamond, on the other hand, we can go out and verify the existence of diamonds. We can pick diamonds up, inspect them, and study their geological features and make-up. We know they exist. They are real. This, then, is a *real link* between the word and the word's referent.[29] It's real because the link between the object and the object's description *really* exists in the *real* world.

Craig Lee Duckett, an advocate for ignosticism, states it another way.

> Without pointing to words, without relying on word associations, what can you tell me about God? If you can't tell me anything without referring back to word associations, then the word associations themselves—omnipotent, omniscient, omnipresent, and omnibenevolent—are meaningless since they also are composed of associations that cannot be proven and are nowhere in evidence.[30]

Therefore, in order to talk about God as a *real* being, as something extant, the burden is on the theist to show the *real link* between the object "God" and its referent in reality, just as string theorists must show the real link between their concept of vibrating strings and

---

[29] A *real link* is part of the theory of Referential Justification where two separate representations can reference the same object (hence referent) which, consequently, allows the two definitions to converge allowing the representations to become one and the same. God definitions universally fail this basic justification. See figure 1 in the Appendix.

[30] Craig Lee Duckett, "Ignosticism and Theological noncognitivism," available online at: http://www.control-z.com/czp/pgs/ignostic.html#top

its relationship to reality.

As we saw in the previous chapter, we have discovered that there is no presently reliable reference point to demonstrate the term "God" relates back to anything that exists in the real world. Just like those mysteriously illusive vibrating strings which elude detecting, seemingly existing only in the minds of theoretical physicists, God is also a type of abstraction which appears to only exist in the minds of religious believers. Thus, until a *real link* for God can be demonstrated, we must concede to the fact that the term "God" is confined to the *conceptual* realm of ideas (not things which exist apart from them).

Referential justification becomes necessary when talking about things which supposedly exist because it helps us overcome an annoying semantic hurdle that arises out of how one talks about something which only has a *conceptual link* as if it were real.[31]

Without proving there is any real link to the thing itself, all one has done is provide an incoherent description by calling something *imaginary* real. Imaginary-real things cannot possibly exist. This is a semantic confusion we need to be aware of, especially when discussing the God-concept, since God is

---

[31] A *conceptual link* is part of the theory of Referential justification where two separate representations share a template (i.e., Omnipresent [Person] = cognitive powers), but unable to justify a *real link* with the object, the definitions diverge rather than converge. See figure 2 in the Appendix.

something many believers like to pretend is real even though it seems more likely that God is an imaginary construct in the same way that the aforementioned vibrating strings in string theory are imaginary constructs.

Inevitably, semantic confusion impacts the nature of the religious discourse and the conversation about God. Apologists have capitalized on it and have ingeniously used it to their advantage. A good example of semantic confusion being masterfully employed by a theologian can be found in the debate between the British philosopher Stephen Law and the American Christian theologian William Lane Craig.[32]

In their debate, Craig showed that he didn't want to give an inch in how he defined God. He kept reiterating unjustified theological terms, such as God being transcendent, immutable, timeless, etc., all of which clearly relied on pre-existing theological templates that ascribe ostensible attributes to God. Once again, we must be made aware that this falls in line with the religious practice of ritualistic naming—i.e., God is imagined to be this or that—and not any valid method of describing—God is tested and observed to be this and that. Furthermore, Craig's failure to provide any real link, hence referential support, for God meant that

---

[32] The full 2011 Westminster debate between William Lane Craig and Stephen Law can be viewed online at:

http://www.youtube.com/watch?feature=player_embedded&v=w7FhphWDokA

God, as Craig defined it, is by definition an abstraction and not something which exists. Ironically enough, one of Craig's principle claims was that God really exists.

If I were taking to task the theologian, I would say, look here, for me to take your question about the existence of God seriously you have to demonstrate to me that your definition of God is coherent, and what's more, that it is about something real and not merely a figment of the religious imagination. One possible way you might choose to do this is by showing us a *real link* between your description of God and the real world referent from which you derived said description. Surely, if I can give you a Granny Smith apple, which *really* exists, then I have established the real link between the term and its referent in the real world. What's more, you can verify it for yourself, and our descriptions will match up accordingly.

It really is that simple. All the theist has to do is provide a valid description of God which passes the test of Referential justification, thereby establishing a real link between the thing itself and its description, which we may then verify and presumably find agreement. This, however, has not happened.

Needless to say, this places the theist in a difficult position. She will either have to admit she is talking about a concept, or else, she will retreat to well-worn apologetic defenses, invoke semantic confusion, throw incoherent and meaningless terms around, and incorrectly call the *God-concept* "real." Or she may simply say we cannot disprove metaphysical realities beyond our epistemic purview; even though this has nothing to say about how she is deriving her definitions.

In the end, what William Lane Craig seems to do, as apologists often do, is force everyone to accept their definition of God regardless of whether or not it is justifiable, meaningful, or even coherent. Like other theists, he is willing to deny any competing definitions for the same concept so as not to have to be burdened with the bothersome task of justifying his chosen definition of God.

Semantic confusion is a red flag and a good indicator that something is askew in the logic of the language and gives us good reason to pause. By keeping God confined to a semantic purgatory—a gray zone in which God can be defined and redefined any which way the theist sees fit, but at the same time, allowing the theist to deny any definition of God which doesn't fit their ever changing scale of what the term means or could possibly mean—the term "God" can come to mean anything the theist desires.

Regardless of how a definition, term, or word is defined, a higher order of justification is always required to establish a substantive theory of meaning, otherwise we could not claim to be talking about anything with meaning. If our words ceased to have meaning then our definitions would fail us and we'd be stuck in a permanent state of semantic confusion.

Ignosticism along with Referential justification

seeks to avoid this knotty semantic confusion by establishing three things. They are as follows:

1. It seeks to show a real link exists over a conceptual—or else provides the opposite—by showing there is no real link at all, but merely a conceptual link;

2. It seeks to define the logical and lexical meanings and investigates their limits;

3. Finally, it establishes the truth condition of the terms being used (since to know this condition is equivalent to knowing the meaning of the term).

Subsequently, following these three steps when thinking about our definitions does away with the constant semantic confusion which is employed by theists and theologians alike who constantly shift their meanings and habitually redefine their terms. Minus the present confusion which makes most religious talk about God ambiguous at best, we now have a way to bring focus to our definitions and determine their relationship either to the real or the conceptual, thereby being able to contextualize them given an adequate understanding of their apposite meaning.

6

POSSIBLE OBJECTIONS

UPON SHARING WHAT THE POSITION IGNOSTICISM entails, I often run into those who assume that their definition of God is true based on nothing more than authority, ascendancy, or ubiquity whereas—for no justifiable reason I can discern—all other competing beliefs are somehow counterfeit. When I ask them how they know this, they usually appeal to the authority of their church, their faith, or their prejudice, e.g. all other religions are wrong because their holy book says so, or because their religious leader warned them about false prophets, etc. These people cannot be taken seriously because they have effectively stated they refuse to test their claims against other competing claims. How do they know their claim is in fact true? They can't.

What if, and this is the exact consideration they

refuse to consider, they are mistaken? What if Brahma is the true Supreme Being and all Christians are wrong? What if the description Hindus give of Brahma better represents reality as we know it? If they never held their idea of God up against any other competing ideas, well, they would never know if they were wrong. As such, claiming they are right (insofar as their understanding of God goes) without first testing to make sure requires us to ignore their claims because their method in how they have come to these conclusions about supposed truths is demonstrably flawed.

So simply "knowing" is not enough to counter the challenge of ignosticism.

Another objection I often hear is the parable of the four blind men and the elephant. The parable goes like this: the first blind, feeling the elephant's sharp pointed tusk, concludes it is a spear. The second blind man, taking a hold of the animal's tail, concludes it is a rope. A third blind man, holding the elephant's massive leg believes it to be a tree trunk. A fourth blind man, feeling only the elephant's thick trunk believes it to be a garden hose.

Now, many posit this parable as a good metaphor for how other religions might all grasp God in some degree, each perceiving a small part of the bigger whole. The idea is that even though their definitions may clash, ultimately they are all on the right track. They all are experiencing *different* aspects of God, but it is still God in some capacity or another.

On my blog *Advocatus Atheist*, a theist reader wrote in to contend the ignostic position, stating:

> Your first view in Ignosticism is impossible to satisfy. How can a finite being provide a "coherent definition" of an infinite being? We are not capable of it.

My response, in kind, was:

> All you have done, it seems, is semantically twist the definition of God to mean that which is incomprehensible. In which case you void any and all purported experiences of God because you couldn't comprehend them. This is exactly what ignosticism concerns itself with.

He denied the observation and claimed:

> No, that's not what I've done at all. I can certainly have valid experiences with an infinite God; while I might have difficulty articulating such an experience, I cannot and never would claim to be able to define Him, confine Him to my limited view or know more than an infinitesimal fraction of who or what God is ... What I can do is be humble in the face of God - not an attitude I find in many atheists (or in your case, ignosticists?).

In fact, it's not hard to see that is exactly what he has

done. He claimed his view is "limited" and that he could only know an "infinitesimal fraction of who or what God is" but this is exactly taking God to mean something incomprehensible because it is the same as saying, although I have this definition for God, I cannot know God. If this is the case, then how can you have a definition for God?

Reiterating my main points, I responded:

> I would say any experience which you could not learn from is probably an unintelligible experience. In which case, the question would be, is it really God that you believe you are experiencing? How would you know? In a sense you are admitting to know God, or certain attributes of God, via his interaction with you. But this places the burden on you to define God as something coherent, otherwise your entire experience of God proves to be meaningless because you cannot describe it.

> Or do you, perhaps, just like the idea of belief in God so much that you are willing to obscure his very entity by claiming your experiences, albeit real, simply cannot be understood because whatever God is, and however he chooses to reveal himself, is as mysterious as he is transcendent? Well, then, if that's how you wish to define God, then there is simply nothing to talk about.

But if you wish to start talking about the experiences and how God reveals himself to you, then you are dealing with experiences which can be cognitively understood, thereby revealing aspects of God which, by description of the experience, are comprehensible. But you can't have it both ways.

A seriously thoughtful person who was following the debate chimed in and asked:

So, basically the problem of defining God as incomprehensible is that it makes God incoherent by definition? ... I guess one could ask the theist how they know God is incomprehensible ... if he is truly incomprehensible, how would we even figure that out? If the theist doesn't know what they're worshiping, then they are just as agnostic as any skeptic.

The only objection I can really think of is to say that if a truly infinite God existed in reality, it would be incomprehensible to us, with our limited minds. Therefore the theist would say that it is arrogant of us to assume we need to define God, since we can never know what he is. What do you think of this line of argument?

I think his main point bears repeating.
"So, basically the problem of defining God as

incomprehensible is that it makes God incoherent by definition?"

Excellent! Yes, exactly. If God is truly incomprehensible then the experiences believers attribute to God are by extension unintelligible and therefore meaningless. To claim God is incomprehensible, since we have finite minds, is to deny our cognitive ability to understand infinitely complex minds. I do not see any evidence to suggest finite minds cannot detect infinite minds.

At this point, the theist may offer this rebuttal.

"Ah-ha! But you see, that is my point. I can recognize God exists, but I cannot understand him, so I cannot describe him to you."

However, if this truly was the case, then there wouldn't be theology, since by its very definition, theology is the study of God. I do not know of any religions without a theology. In fact, I would argue that in order for a religion to be classified as a religion, it would first require a relatable theology.

This is where most theists get hung up. Many simply assume our minds are capable of detecting the infinite mind of God through our experience of God, thereby recognizing the experience as tangible, but then, in the same breath, they turn around and say whatever that experience contains in terms of information cannot be understood due to God's incomprehensible nature.

The claim that God is incomprehensible to us

therefore *voids the experience of God.* As our thoughtful reader mentioned, there is no proper way to test what we are experiencing would be God, or something from our imaginations that we, in our inferior state of mind, mistook for God. Or something else entirely.

So we come to see that the argument of finite minds being unable to detect infinite minds, or that it is impossible to define an incomprehensible God, or give adequate description of our experience of God, are all self-refuting claims, and therefore cannot be cited as objections.

This is usually the point where theologians and theists like to invoke semantic gymnastics, but as we have seen, ignosticism is fully capable of dealing with semantic games. This is where the second part of ignosticism comes into play. If, for example, the semantic trick is to make God an unfalsifiable abstraction, such as defining him as transcendent, immutable, eternal, etc., then ignosticism takes the theological noncognitivist position.

According to theological noncognitivism, one cannot define God in terms of God. It is circular reasoning, and therefore results in begging the question. Therefore, the definition of God is predicated on a fallacy and is rendered invalid.

What about the doctrine of Divine simplicity? This is the final objection to ignosticism I will address here.

Divine simplicity is the theological position that

God is without parts. The general idea being that the being of God is identical to the "attributes" of God. As such, the characteristics of omnipresence, goodness, truth, eternity, etc. are identical to God's *being*, not qualities that make up that being, nor abstract entities inhering in God as in a substance.

The problem is Divine simplicity fails for the very objection Wittgenstein raised early on. These attributes wouldn't be effective descriptions of God, grammatically speaking, they would merely fall into the category of being alternative 'names' for the same thing. In which case, they complicate the idea of an ultimately simplistic description of God, because if such a being existed, such 'names' would not be needed to describe it—as it would be maximally simplistic.

St. Augustine also ran into this problem with how he defined God. As Wittgenstein observed:

> Augustine, we might say, does describe a system of communication; only not everything that we call language is this system. And one has to say this in several cases where the question arises "Will that description do or not?" The answer is: "Yes, it will, but only for this narrowly circumscribed area, not for the whole of what you were purporting to describe."[33]

---

[33] Wittgenstein, *Philosophical Investigations*, p.6e.

What this observation entails is that in order to describe God adequately, in order to provide a description which will encompass the whole of what one purports to be describing, more than a simplistic definition "God" is required. This is why theologians love to assign "attributes" to God. Even calling God "maximally simple" is a type of descriptor or attribute.

Unable to assign these descriptors to God however, theologians would have nothing to talk about. As a result, our understanding of God must always be greater than a minimal description, otherwise we could have no understanding of God.

Finally, the only real objection to ignosticism in my mind is the position is that we should not be so quick to try to define God (should such a being exist). The assumption here is that if God is real, then over time our experiences will line up enough that our definitions will eventually become congruent with one another.

Recall the elephant in the room analogy. If our common denominator of experience was met, then all the blind men would simply shift position and upon seeing that one another's descriptions of the elephant were indeed valid, would simply reformulate their descriptions. Eventually, the blind men's descriptions would all converge, based on this common denominator of shared experience. We should expect the same with respect to God—if God is something that exists in reality and interacts with us on the level of real world experience. Therefore, we should let our experience bring us into a better understanding with regard to the question of how we might best define God.

The only problem I have with this assumption is that, until a universalized definition of God can be identified, we are still in the dark as to which, if any of the remaining definitions, are accurately describing this God or not. That is, maybe one of the blind men has wondered off and has begun feeling up a lamp post. Evidently the problem of incoherent and meaningless definitions does not go away. So we would have to wait until all definitions unified, or coalesced if you will, into a universally accepted description of God, and this is the definition we could begin to talk about as having any relevance.

Not having a unified, universal, description for God we are again without a concise working definition, and this takes us right back to the default position of agnosticism—the position that we lack the requisite information (knowledge) to adequately speak about God's existence—and thus belief in God would not be warranted.

Without the warrant to believe, and belief in God being meaningless, what alternative is there?

7

IGNOSTICISM & ATHEISM

WHEN IT COMES TO GOD, I REALIZE, there are many people who say they have experienced God, that they have had real perceptible encounters, and that they can measure God in terms of the frequency of these shared experiences. The problem with this is not everyone experiences God in the same way. What's more, if God were in any way real, we'd have a referent and all of our definitions of God would match up exactly. They do not.

The problem, as I see it, is the fact that many believers are simply taking their definitions of God for granted. But this susceptibility isn't confined to just how they think and talk about God. Consider the Christian predisposition to believe that Christianity best explains reality as they see it. As Bud Uzoras, rationalist and author of the blog *Dead-Logic*, has keenly observed, such a belief seemingly begs the question.

> "Why do I think Christianity is true? Because it best explains reality." Saying it "best explains reality" is basically a restatement of "Christianity is true"... That is clearly "begging the question" in the correct sense of the phrase ("petitio principia" to be exact).[34]

In effect, Christians who define God by using the attributes of God to explain God are also begging the question. Like the theologian we talked about earlier, who resorts to describing God as transcendent, immutable, eternal, all-knowing, and so forth, all we have is yet another a case of begging the question.

Begging the question is a type of fallacy in which the conclusion is taken for granted in the premise. In other words, for the same reason a Christian or Muslim might take for granted their faith that God is true, they are also taking for granted that the term 'God' means exactly what they want it to mean, in every possible

---

[34] Bud Uzoras is the author of the blog *Dead-Logic*, where he talks about, among other things, how to improve our critical thinking skills and become better skeptics. The above quote was taken from a discussion he had with a Christian friend, which can be read online at:

http://dead-logic.blogspot.jp/2013/07/more-chatting-with-chris-chin.html

situation, so that when they talk about God they assume that everyone will, like them, know exactly what they mean. But if you have a different definition of God, or no definition at all, as is the case with nonbelievers, then it clearly is a case of taking for granted your definition of 'God' is the only definition worth considering. It's not.

Where does atheism enter into the equation, you wonder? Well, it's like this. If all our definitions of God do in fact prove to be incoherent, then it's simply meaningless to talk about God—because it would be the same as talking about nothing. What this implies is that we never had access to any real referent which could yield the information required to form an accurate description of what God is, how he functions, and what his properties are. Knowing this we can conclude one of two things. Either there is no God, or if by some small chance there is, he is impossible to detect (e.g., see the *argument from divine hiddenness*)—in which case— God may as well not exist in the first place.

Realizing this the theist has no choice but to revert to agnosticism, admitting that they do not know the first thing about God should he exist, and concede to the ignostic claim that they presume too much.

Let's not forget the other possibility that God exists *only* as a concept and nothing more, and if this is the case then it is meaningless to talk about something imaginary as extant. Simply put, the abstract concept called "God" is imaginary and therefore nonexistent. As such, there would be nothing further to talk about since this is already the atheist's claim, and it's a reasonable one at that.

So you see, the two possible consequences of ignosticism are that God, should he exist, is either undetectable or there is no God at all. Atheism takes the latter position and therefore ignosticism can be used as a justification for the reasonableness of atheism.

Meanwhile, if by some infinitesimally small chance God should exist as some imperceptible entity, then atheism is still the more rational position as it assumes nothing about God, whereas the theist continues to make the mistake of assuming far too much. But if God is truly imperceptible, that means both atheists and theists would know the same amount about God, namely nothing, so what could the theist possibly be basing their information on other than conjecture?

This demonstrates that between theism and atheism, atheism comes out as the more prudent theological position of the two.

Of course, taking the position that there is no God or gods often is accompanied by the challenge to dissuade the believer of their deepest felt convictions and prove that their intuition is somehow mistaken. Ask the question "Does God exist?" and answer it with "No, there is no God," and the theist wants to know how the atheist could possibly come to such a conclusion if they are unable to disprove God.

The atheist at once has to justify her position. She can do this by taking the position of the empiricist and raising the objection that the challenge of providing sufficient evidence to believe has not been met.

Subsequently, a standard fair theistic objection to the naturalistic empirical worldview is to say the atheist is being overly materialistic. That God is not of the material world. Accordingly, the atheist is stuck, with only a prudent theological position but not one which can positively be demonstrated in their favor. But the atheist who adopts the ignostic position can, and this is the best part, positively deny the existence of God.

Ask the question "Does God exist?" and the theist has to come up with a demonstration for God which is reliable enough to provide an adequate description and one that doesn't devolve into an abstract conceptualization. An ignostic-atheist is content to dismiss unproved concepts. After all, there would be no reason not to!

Non-belief in abstract, incoherent, God-conceptualizations which, as traditionally defined, prove to be meaningless, if not downright unintelligible, makes perfect sense to the atheist. It's as Wittgenstein once remarked, "What cannot be imagined cannot even be talked about."[35]

Most believers, on the other hand, never take it this

<hr />

[35] Ludwig Wittgenstein, Notebooks 1914-1916. Journal entry (p. 84e); October 12, 1916.

far. Rather, they are content to settle on the religious template that best works for them, ostensible attributes and all. At the same time, theists will continue to ignore the bothersome consequences of semantic confusion, and will take it for granted that their definition of God might not be justifiable. That, at the end of the day, the very word they think describes something actually doesn't describe anything at all.

8

PSYCHOLOGY OF RELIGION

ONE FINAL QUESTION WE NEED TO ADDRESS is where do we derive our concepts of God from? It seems to me that ignosticism, although works splendidly to analyze the coherence of a term, cannot seek to explain why the terms themselves are superfluous, except to say that conceptualizations have a natural tendency to diverge when rooted in subjective experience. But why are there multiple conceptualizations in the first place? Why are there different God-theories?

Personally, I feel there are perhaps good explanations to be found in a slightly better understanding of human psychology. In fact, I have found that psychology, sociology, and anthropology each provide a surplus of reasons as to why our ideas of God and personal religious experience are so varied.

I think we can agree that most people acquire their

religious beliefs in one of two ways. First, beliefs are predominantly the product of our either being born into a faith, usually the faith of our parents,[36] or they are the product of our being indoctrinated early on as children—as a form of cultural assimilation. The Great Agnostic Robert G. Ingersoll, speaking on indoctrination early on, stated that

> It is hard to overestimate the influence of early training in the direction of superstition. You first teach children that a certain book is true—that it was written by God himself—that to question its truth is a sin, that to deny it is a crime, and that should they die without believing that book they will be forever damned without benefit of clergy. The consequence is that long before they read that book, they believe it to be true. When they do read it their minds are wholly unfitted to investigate its claim. They accept it as a matter of course.... In this way the brain of man has become a kind of palimpsest upon which, and over the writings of nature, superstition has scrawled her countless lies.[37]

---

[36] Having religious parents factors in greatly as to what a person's religious disposition will be. Usually, a person's religious attitudes will align with the religious teachings of their parents. Studies have found that this inherited disposition can be genetically acquired. See Michael Shermer, *The Believing Brain*, p. 169.

[37] Robert G. Ingersoll. From "Individuality," in *Reason Against Blasphemy*, p. 300.

What this means is that often times before we can even read or write many of us have been inundated with religious belief, archaic rituals, and superstition. Nearly every religious believer in the world has been indoctrinated and inculcated into their respective belief systems in one way or another.

Of course, this doesn't mean there aren't those who have made a reasoned choice to believe in God, or in deciding this faith over that one, but they are few and far between. Ingersoll was right, we find that it is the early instigation of religious thinking into the minds of young children by which most people acquire their religious beliefs.

Knowing this, we come to see that most peoples' understandings of God are no more sophisticated than that of a child's. This is due to the early training, where they were instilled with their religious beliefs, including the belief in God, before their brains could properly mature and before they could critically evaluate complex philosophical questions.

More notably, perhaps, is the fact that they did not come to these beliefs on their own accord. They were told what to believe. They were told what to believe by their parents, their elders in their community, their religious leaders, and sometimes even their teachers (even though telling children what to think isn't a valid form of teaching, technically speaking). Most children have nonstop cultural and peer pressure for them to accept religious beliefs coming at them from every angle. So, in their powerlessness, they simply believe what they are told to believe. It doesn't help matters that religions of all kinds have traditionally punished those who challenged their authority and have frequently discouraged uncertainty and skepticism.

Besides, if it were easy to reason oneself into religion, more people would be doing it instead of just accepting their religious beliefs as a matter of faith. But reasoning is hard. Reasoning requires us to become familiar with other religions and religious concepts. It requires us to compare and contrast multiple belief systems. It requires us to be able to evaluate these belief systems, recognize their strengths and weaknesses, and ultimately requires a fair bit of critical evaluation.

The bottom line is believing is easy. Thinking is hard.

Most children cannot perform a deeper level of critical reasoning. Their brains simply aren't matured enough to handle complex analytical tasks. It's only after we have become thinking adults can we properly evaluate the claims of religion.

Once having become adults however, suffice to say, most do not go back to re-evaluate their inherited religious beliefs. I feel the reasons most people do not take the time to reconsider their religious beliefs once they become capable of doing so is pretty straight forward. As adults, most people's lives become extremely busy with things like work, raising kids, paying the mortgage, and all the rest of life's problems.

Then there is the old ranch hand's maxim that if it ain't broke, don't fix it. Forget any improvements, just take it as is. Why? Because improving it would take real work. It would require you to take it all apart, figure out how to make it even better, and then put it all together again. Indeed, this may be the primary reason people don't go back and take another look at their beliefs. It is, to be honest, too darn hard.

Evaluating anything takes time and energy. Most people simply do not have such luxuries. As a father raising a family and working two jobs, I can sympathize. Sometimes the days simply aren't long enough.

Besides this, our beliefs are not as static as we'd like to think. As the American scientist and skeptic Michael Shermer explains:

> Belief change comes from a combination of personal psychological readiness and a deeper social and cultural shift in the underlying zeitgeist, which is affected in part by education but is more the product of larger and harder-to-define political, economic, religious, and social changes.[38]

But even so, if a religious adult truly wanted to make an up-close examination of their faith, all they would have to do it set a little time aside and begin to investigate the questions which arise from their natural

---

[38] Michael Shermer, *The Believing Brain*, p. 4

borne curiosity.

However, I feel I should warn that caution is necessary, because studies have shown that the more knowledgeable you become about religion, and the better you get at critical thinking, the less religious you will become.[39] Which is another reason most people do not typically reason their way into religion.

All this simply to explain a phenomenon. Not only do people tend *not* to assess their acquired childhood beliefs, but not having re-evaluated them most people are stuck with a childlike understanding of God, theology, and perhaps equally of their religion as a whole.

Knowing this we might wonder, if people are stuck with a naïve understanding of God, how are we getting such complexity in the type of God beliefs that are prolific in human culture?

The evolutionary psychologist and anthropologist Pascal Boyer has suggested that

> Most accounts of the origins of religion amount to one of the following suggestions: human minds demand explanations, human hearts seek comfort, human society requires order, human intellect is illusion-prone.[40]

[39] Will M. Gervais and Ara Norenzayan, "Analytic Thinking Promotes Religious Disbelief," Science 27, April 2012, Vol. 336 no. 6080 pp. 493-496.

[40] Pascal Boyer, *Religion Explained*, p.3

Being prone to superstition. Wanting to understand the world. Desiring a nourishing form of comfort that will make our lives more fulfilling. Seeking the answers, not on our own, but together as communities, becoming united in the pursuit of figuring out the bigger questions of why we're here and what our purpose is. All this nicely predicts how we might get such a variety of religious experiences, religions, and definitions of God.

But having a belief, or a definition for that matter, isn't enough to claim that these beliefs and definitions constitute any kind of reality. After all, even the largest world religion could still be mistaken. Ubiquity of belief must never be mistaken for biology. Like-beliefs must not be mistaken for universal truths. In order to make the sorts of wide-sweeping claims that the religious tend to make, one has to realize, all their proving is still ahead of them.

The fact that many religious people experience the same type of experience(s) doesn't, I'm afraid, prove these experiences are in any way true. At least, not true in the objective sense. Certainly individual experiences are subjectively true, and appear true to the individual experiencing them. This is fine, because personal biases can be tested for. But the mistake I see all too often is when a believer makes the claim that what is true for them must also be true for everyone else. Such claims are often the result of poor critical thinking, and sometimes even mass delusion. Such examples are well documented in cases of cult behavior, from belief in UFOs and alien abductions to conspiracy theories, and from religious nuns to religious nutters.

Therefore, as thinking, reasoning people we must heed the wisdom of the late great Carl Sagan and realize that extraordinary claims require extraordinary evidence, and if something can be claimed without evidence, such as an invisible dragon living in our garage, then it can be dismissed without evidence.

Given our understanding of how our minds are seemingly hardwired to be superstitious, and seeing as how religion caters to this trait in human behavior, my hope is that for those serious about these philosophical questions, and others like them, that they might take the time to consider the ignostic position.

Until the religious believer can formulate a valid justification for their terms then I am afraid there simply isn't anything to talk about. Not really, anyway.

So you want to know, "Does God exist?"

Well, "What do you mean by *God*?"

FINIS

APPENDIX

Referential Justification
Illustrations

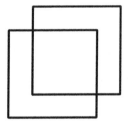

Figure 1

Real Link

Definition 1⇨Real Link⇨Object⇦Real Link⇦Definition 2
Perspective 1⇨Convergence⇦Perspective 2

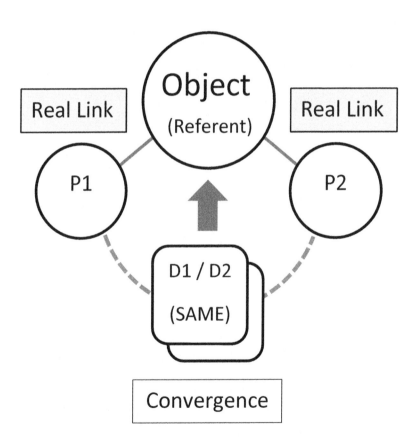

Figure 2

Conceptual Link

Definition 1⇐Conceptual⇨Concept⇐Conceptual⇨Definition 2
Perspective 1⇐Divergence⇨Perspective 2

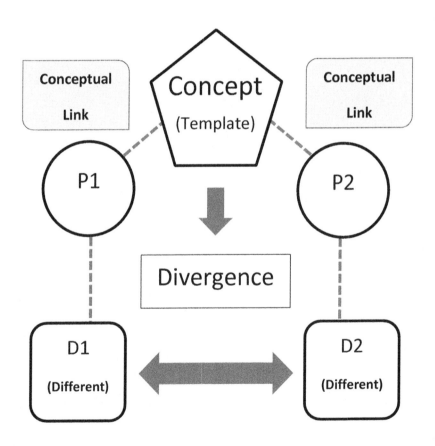

BIBLIOGRAPHY

Asch, S.E. "Effects of group pressure upon the modification and distortion of judgment." In H. Guetzkow (ed.) *Groups, leadership and men*. Pittsburgh, PA: Carnegie Press, 1951.

———. "Opinions and social pressure." *Scientific American*, 193 (1955): 31-35.

Bering, Jesse Bering. *The Belief Instinct: The Psychology of Souls, Destiny, and the Meaning of Life*. New York: W.W. Norton, 2012.

Berns, G.S., et al., "Neurobiological Correlates of Social Conformity and Independence During Mental Rotation," *Biological Psychiatry*, 58 (2005): 245-253.

Boyer, Pascal. *Religion Explained*. New York: Basic Books, 2001.

Conifer, Steven J. "Theological Noncognitivism Examined," *The Interlocutor: Sewanee Undergraduate Philosophical Review* 4 (2002): Retrieved July, 2013.
http://web.archive.org/web/20090326144947/http://www.sewanee.edu/philosophy/Journal/Archives/2002/Conifer.htm

Demetriou, Andreas, W. Doise, and K.F.M. van Lieshout, eds., "Cognitive development," *Life-span developmental psychology* (1998): 179-269. London: Wiley, 1998.

Demetriou, Andreas, and Athanassios Raftopoulos. "Modeling the Developing Mind: From Structure to Change." *Developmental Review* 19 (1999): 319-368.

Doolittle, Mike. "A Slow Crawl Toward Ontological Naturalism," *The A-Unicornist*, published April 11, 2011. Retrieved July 2013.
http://www.theaunicornist.com/2011/04/slow-crawl-toward-ontological.html

Drange, Theodore. "Atheism, Agnosticism, Noncognitivism" by Theodore Drange," Internet Infidels, *Secular Web Library* (1998): Retrieved July, 2013.
http://www.infidels.org/library/modern/theodore_drange/definition.html

Duckett, Craig Lee. "Ignosticism and Theological noncognitivism," Control-Z.com. Retrieved June 2013.
http://www.control-z.com/czp/pgs/ignostic.html#top

Gervais, Will M., and Ara Norenzayan. "Analytic Thinking Promotes Religious Disbelief," Science 27 (2012): 493-496.

Hein, George E. "Constructivist Learning Theory," presented at the CECA conference, Israel, 1991.

Ingersoll, Robert G. "Individuality," in *Reason Against Blasphemy*. Hungry Word Publications, 2012.

Kahneman, Daniel. *Thinking, Fast and Slow*. New York: Farrar, Straus and Giroux, 2011.

Kurtz, Paul. *The New Skepticism*. New York: Prometheus Books, 1992.

Law, Stephen, and William Lane Craig. "Does God Exist?" Westminster debate, 2011. *YouTube*: Retrieved July 2013. http://www.youtube.com/watch?feature=player_embedded&v=w7FhphWDokA

Martin, Michael. *Atheism: A Philosophical Justification*. Philadelphia: Temple University Press, 1990.

Martin, Michael, and Ricki Monnier, eds. *The Improbability of God*. NY: Prometheus Books, 2006.

Nishapuri, Muslim ibn al-Hajjaj. *Sahih Muslim*, 35:6475.

Nonaka, Ikujiro, and Hirotaka Takeuchi. *The Knowledge-Creating Company: How Japanese Companies Create the Dynamics of Innovation*. New York: Oxford University Press, 1995.

Schellenberg, J.L. "Would a loving God hide from anyone?" in Solomon, Robert, and Douglas McDermid, eds., London: *Introducing Philosophy for Canadians*, Oxford University Press, 2011.

Sherif, M. "A study of some social factors in perception," *Archives of Psychology*, 27 (1935): 17-22.

Shermer, Michael. *The Believing Brain: From Ghosts and Gods to Politics and Conspiracies—How We Construct Beliefs and Reinforce them as Truths*. New York: Macmillan, 2011.

Snobelen, Stephen D. "Isaac Newton, heretic: the strategies of a Nicodemite." *British Journal for the History of Science* 32 (1999): 381–419.

Steffe, Leslie P., and Jerry Gale. *Constructivism in Education*. New Jersey: Routledge, 2012.

Tremblay, Francois. "List of thousands of dead gods," *Graveyard of the Gods* (2005): Retrieved July, 2013. http://www.graveyardofthegods.org/deadgods/listofgods.html

Uzoras, Bud. "More Chatting with Chris Chin," *Dead-Logic*, published July 14, 2013. Retrieved July, 2013. http://dead-logic.blogspot.jp/2013/07/more-chatting-with-chris-chin.html

Wittgenstein, Ludwig. *Philosophical Investigations, Fourth edition*. West Sussex: Wiley-Blackwell, 2009.

Zull, James. *The art of changing the brain: Enriching the practice of teaching by exploring the biology of learning*. Sterling, VA: Stylus Publishing, L.L.C., 2002.

ABOUT THE AUTHOR

TRISTAN VICK GRADUATED FROM MONTANA State University with degrees in English Literature and Asian Cultural Studies. He speaks fluent Japanese and lives in Japan with his wife and daughter. When he's not commuting on the train or teaching English he spends his time reading, writing, blogging, and eating sara-udon. He is the author of the popular zombie series *Bitten: A Resurrection Thriller*, *Bitten 2: Land of the Rising Dead*, and the upcoming *Bitten 3: Kingdom of the Living Dead*. He is editor of the non-fiction collections *Reason Against Blasphemy* and *Seasons of Freethought* which collects together the freethought works of G.W. Foote and Robert G. Ingersoll. You can learn more about the author or contact him at: **www.tristanvick.com**

Made in the USA
Coppell, TX
17 March 2021

51895013R00056